About the Author

Mr. Sagar Salunke has 10 years of experience in automation testing including QTP(UFT) and Selenium Webdriver in Java and C#. He has worked on large investment banking projects in tier-1 Software Companies in India, USA, UK, Australia and Switzerland.

He has designed automation frameworks in Selenium with C#.Net that is widely used in the IT industry.

His hobbies include travelling to new tourist places, watching basketball, cricket and learning latest technological stuff.

0

A special note of Thanks to My Wife

I would like to dedicate this book to my lovely wife Priyanka for loving me so much and helping me write this book. Without her support, this book would not have been a reality.

Preface

These days lot of web applications are being developed to meet the growing demands of business.

So testing these applications is a big challenge. Automating test scenarios has become almost inevitable to reduce the overall cost and fast regression testing.

Selenium webdriver is the best open source testing framework that can be used to automate the testing activities in web application project.

In this book I have included all webdriver concepts with examples in C#.Net.

Table of Contents

1. SELENIUM Basics

In this chapter you will get familiar with selenium Webdriver. You will also learn about the Installation of Visual Studio Express edition along with Selenium Webdriver.We will also write a simple C#.Net program with selenium webdriver.

1.1. What is Selenium?

Selenium is the open source web application testing framework released under apache license. Selenium can be installed on

1. Windows
2. Linux
3. Macintosh.

It supports programming in many languages as mentioned below.

1. C#.Net (also vb.net, J#)
2. Java
3. PHP
4. Ruby
5. Python
6. Perl

1.2. What is selenium webdriver?

Selenium WebDriver is the successor to Selenium RC. In earlier versions of selenium we needed Selenium RC server to execute the test scripts.

Now we can use webdriver to execute the tests on particular browser. For each browser we have a separate web driver which accepts the selenium commands and drives the browser under test.

1.3. Browsers supported by Selenium.

Below is the list of browsers supported by the selenium webdriver.

1. Internet Explorer
2. Google Chrome
3. Firefox
4. Opera
5. Safari

Please note that for each browser, there is a separate web driver implementation.

1.4. Choosing technology for selenium.

As mentioned earlier, there are lot of languages that can be used for selenium scripting. Choosing the language depends upon the below factors.

1. Skill Set of employees in the organisation.
2. Training required on specific language.

I have selected C#.Net as a programming language for selenium scripting. So in this book you will see all examples in C#.Net only. But the same applies to other languages with some syntactical differences.

1.5. Installing selenium with C#.Net.

Well – Now let us understand the installation steps in selenium.

The list of Softwares you will need is given below.

1. Microsoft Visual Studio Express Edition
   http://www.visualstudio.com/en-us/downloads/download-visual-studio-vs
2. Selenium C#.Net API (dll file)
   @http://docs.seleniumhq.org/download/
3. Web driver for Chrome (exe file)
   @https://code.google.com/p/selenium/downloads/list

If you want to test web applications on the Internet Explorer, you will have to download Internet Explorer driver exe file.

Once you have these softwares with you, You can follow below steps.

- Open C# 2010 express.
- Create a new project with name SampleTest in it.
- Go to project properties, right click and select add references. Browse to the dll file you have downloaded in the 2 step.
- click ok.

You can take help of the visual studio expert on how to do this.

Below image shows how to configure the visual studio for selenium webdriver project.

Open the visual studio and from the file menu select **New Project.**

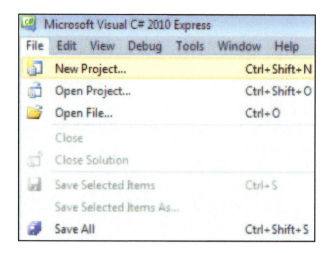

Figure 1 - Create new Project in C# Visual Studio

After you click on new project, you will see New Project window where you have to select the Application Type. We can select Windows Forms Application or Console Based Application.

I have selected Console Based Application. After this, you have to give the name of the project in the bottom section of the window. I have given the name of the project as **SeleniumProject**.

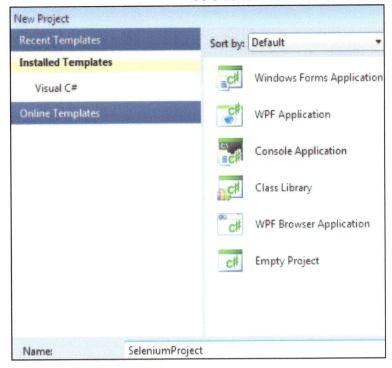

Figure 2 - Select Console Application and Name of Project

When you click on Ok, the project is created for you with sample program class in it. Next figure shows the auto-generated code of the Program Class.
The Program class contains main method which is the entry point for the project execution.

```
SeleniumProject.Program                          ▼  ⚡ Main(string[] args)
using System;
 using System.Collections.Generic;
 using System.Linq;
 using System.Text;

namespace SeleniumProject
 {
    class Program
    {
        static void Main(string[] args)
        {
        }
    }
 }
```

Figure 3 - Auto Generated Code

You can also see the solution explorer at the right hand side showing the file structure of the project and references.

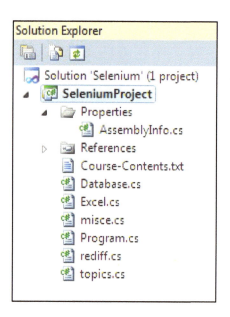

Figure 4 - Solution Explorer showing reference and Classes

Next we have to add the reference of the Selenium Webdriver by right clicking on the project name and selecting **Add Reference option**.

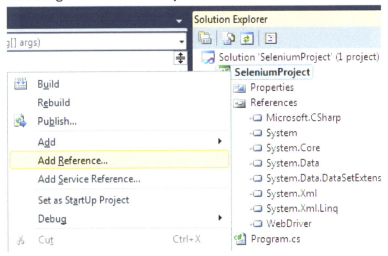

Figure 5 - Add reference of the Selenium Webdriver

You will see Add Reference window as shown below. Select browse tab and choose the webdriver.dll file you downloaded from the internet.

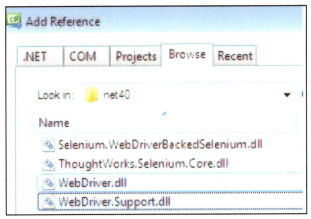

Figure 6 - Select Webdriver.dll

Once you add the webdriver reference, you can use the classes defined in the namespace called OpenQA.Selenium as shown below.

```
Project   Debug   Data   Tools   Window   Help

(string)

Program.cs* X

SeleniumProject.Program                    Main(string[] args)

using System;
using System.Collections.Generic;
using OpenQA.Selenium.Firefox;
using OpenQA.Selenium;
namespace SeleniumProject
{
    class Program
    {
        static void Main(string[] args)
        {
            IWebDriver x = new FirefoxDriver();
            x.Navigate().GoToUrl("http://www.google.com");
            x.Quit();
        }
    }
}
```

Figure 7 - Use selenium classes in the webdriver dll

Above program will launch the firefox browser and open **www.google.com**.

2. First Script in Selenium Webdriver

In this chapter, you will learn how to inspect the web elements in different browsers like IE, Firefox, Google Chrome etc. You will also learn how to write a simple selenium program in C#.Net.

Before I jump to first script in selenium webdriver, let me tell you how you can use developer tool provided by browsers like IE, chrome, firefox while automating the web applications.

Inspecting Elements in Google Chrome.

Google chrome provides very nice tool to inspect the elements on the webpage. You have to just right click on the web element and then select last menu item from the context menu – Inspect. After you click on it, You will see the source code of that element as displayed in below image.

Create a Rediffmail account

Figure 8 - Inspecting Elements in Chrome

Inspecting Elements in Internet Explorer.

Internet Explorer 10 and higher provides the developer
tools from wehre you can inspect the elements on the
webpage. You have to click on the arrow (circled in th red)
and then click on the element on the webpage as
displayed in below image.

Google

India

Google - Developer Tools

File   Find   Disable   View   Outline   Images   Cache   Tools   Validate   Bi

HTML   CSS   Script   Profiler

d-lst-tbb" __jsaction="[object Object]">
'gstl_0 lst-t" id="gs_id0" style="padding-bottom: 0px; padc
action="[object Object]">
action="[object Object]">
lass="gsib_a" id="gs_tti0" __jsaction="[object Object]">
.v id="gs_lc0" style="position: relative;" __jsaction="[obj
<input name="q" title="Search" class="gsfi" id="lst-ib" st
<input disabled="disabled" class="gsfi" id="gs_htif0" aria

Figure 9 - Inspecting Elements in IE

Inspecting Elements in FireFox.

Inspecting elements in firefox is similar to how we do it in chrome. Inspecting elements will help you knowing the attributes of the elements like name, id etc. which in turn can be used in selenium scripts.

Figure 10 - Inspecting element in Firefox

Let us start with scripting right away. Have a look at below example.

2.1. Sample Program

```csharp
using System;
using System.Collections.Generic;
using System.Linq;
using System.Text;
using System.Threading;
using OpenQA.Selenium;
using OpenQA.Selenium.Firefox;
using OpenQA.Selenium.Chrome;
using OpenQA.Selenium.IE;
using OpenQA.Selenium.Support.UI;
using System.Collections.ObjectModel;
namespace Abc
```

```
{
  class Program
  {
static void Main(string[] args)
 {

//IWebDriver x = new
InternetExplorerDriver(@"F:\selenium\csharp");
//IWebDriver x = new FirefoxDriver();
 IWebDriver driver=null;
      try
      {
        driver = new ChromeDriver(@"F:\selenium\csharp");
        driver.Url = "http://www.google.co.in";
        driver.Manage().Window.Maximize();
        driver.Navigate();
       }
      catch(Exception e){
        Console.WriteLine("Exception
....*********"+e.ToString());
      }

      finally{
      Thread.Sleep(2000);
      driver.Quit();
      Console.ReadLine();
       }
    }
  }
}
```

2.2. Explaination

Above program starts with using statement. Using statement is used to bring the classes from particular namespace in the scope of current program.

using OpenQA.Selenium;

For example above statement will bring all classes defined in the OpenQA.Selenium namespace in the context of the current program.

All C#.Net applications have to be included in the namespace. So we have created the namespace called Abc.

Then we have created a class Program. If you are familiar with object oriented programming, you will know the meaning of class. If you are not, you can think of the class as a bluprint of the entity containing properties and methods.

Next statement defines main method which is the starting point for the program.

we have declared new variable driver of the interface type – IwebDriver. Next line starts with try statement. For now, you can ignore this line as I am going to explain this in more detail in exception handling chapter.

driver = new ChromeDriver(@"F:\selenium\csharp");

Above statement will make the driver variable refer to the new browser instance. Please note that ChromeDriver constructor takes the path of the chrome driver.

driver.Url = "http://www.google.co.in";

Above statement will set the url property of the driver to the site we want to open and test.

```
driver.Manage().Window.Maximize();
driver.Navigate();
```

Above 2 statements will maximize the browser window and then open www.google.co.in website in it.

In short we have created the instance of the Chrome webdriver and navigated to the given url.

Below code snippet shows how to create the webdriver instance for the Firefox and IE.

```
IWebDriver x = new
InternetExplorerDriver(@"F:\selenium\csharp");

IWebDriver x = new FirefoxDriver();
```

To launch Internet Explorer, Use below syntax.

```
IWebDriver x = new
InternetExplorerDriver(@"F:\selenium\csharp");
```

When working with Selenium Webdriver and Internet Explorer, ensure that protected mode is enabled for all zones as displayed in below figure.

3. Identifying the elements in SELENIUM

In this chapter, you will learn about different methods of element identification in selenium webdriver like xpath, css, id, name, classname, tagname, linktext, partial link text. You will also come to know the difference between findElement and findElements methods.

As illustrated in the first program, It is very simple to create the webdriver instance and navigate to the webpage. While testing the web applications, we need to perform operations on the webpage like clicking on the link or button, selecting the checkbox or radiobutton, choosing an item from the dropdown etc.

In selenium terminology, all objects in the webpage are treated as webelements. So it is very important to identify the elements first and then perform some operations on them. Selenium provides lot of methods to identify the web elements as mentioned below.

1. Xpath
2. CSS
3. Id
4. Name
5. Class Name
6. Tag Name
7. Link Text
8. Parial Link Text

We are going to look into each of these methods one by one.

Before I jump to the individual identification methods, Let me explain the difference between findElement and findElements.

Well – both the methods can be used to identify the elements from the webpage. The difference is that findElement returns only single matching element while findElements returns all matching web elements from the webpage.

FindElement Example

In below example, findElement method returns the first element with tag – th and prints innertext

```
IWebElement we =
driver.FindElement(By.TagName("th"));

Console.WriteLine(we.Text);
```

FindElements Example

In below example, findElements method returns the collection of all elements with tag – td and prints the innertext of each one. Please note how we have ReadOnlyCollection to store all elements returned by findElements method.

```
ReadOnlyCollection <IWebElement>   mcells
= driver.FindElements(By.TagName("td"));

for (int k=0;k<mcells.Count;k++)
Console.WriteLine (mcells[k].Text));
```

3.1.Xpath

Xpath is the web technology/standard that is used to access elements from the webpage or xml document. Detailed discussion of the xpath is beyond the scope of this book. We will see just simple examples to give you the idea of xpath. You can learn the basics of xpath at http://www.w3schools.com/xpath/xpath_syntax.asp

Examples – Suppose you want to identify the link of which href attribute contains google.

Xpath expression for above example is -
//a[contains(@href,'google')]

Below code will find the first link of which **href** attribute contains google

```
driver.FindElement(By.XPath("//a[contains(@href
,'google')]")).Click();
```

Below table gives some sample xpath expressions.

Find all elements with tag input	`//input`
Find all input tag element having attribute type = 'hidden'	`//input[@type='hidden']`
Find all input tag element having attribute type = 'hidden' and name attribute = 'ren'	`//input[@type='hidden'][@name='ren']`
Find all input tag element with attribute type containing 'hid'	`//input[contains(@type,'hid')]`
Find all input tag element with attribute type starting with 'hid'	`//input[starts-with(@type,'hid')]`
Find all elements having innertext = 'password'	`//*[text()='Password']`
Find all td elements having innertext = 'password'	`//td[text()='Password']`
Find all next siblings of td tag having innertext = 'gender'	`//td[text()='Gender']//following-sibling::*`
Find all elements in the 2nd next sibling of td tag having innertext = 'gender'	`//td[text()='Gender']//following-sibling::*[2]//*`
Find input elements in the 2nd next sibling of td tag having innertext = 'gender'	`//td[text()='Gender']//following-sibling::*[2]//input`
Find the td which contains font element containing the text '12'	`//td[font[contains(text(),'12')]]`
Find all the preceding siblings of the td which contains font element containing the text '12'	`//td[font[contains(text(),'12')]]//preceding-sibling::*`

25

You can also use below tools to learn xpath
1. XPath Checker
2. Firebug.

In google chrome, you can copy the xpath of any element very easily. Below figure shows how we can do it.

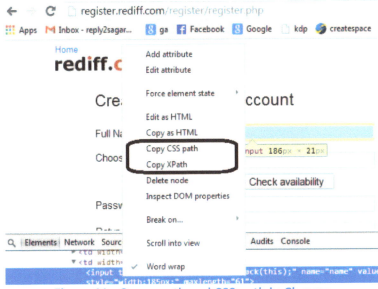

Figure 11 - Copy xpath and CSS path in Chrome

In other browsers like IE and FF also, you will find similar options in developer tools.

You can also use console window to try and test xpath and CSS expressions from the console window provided in chrome.

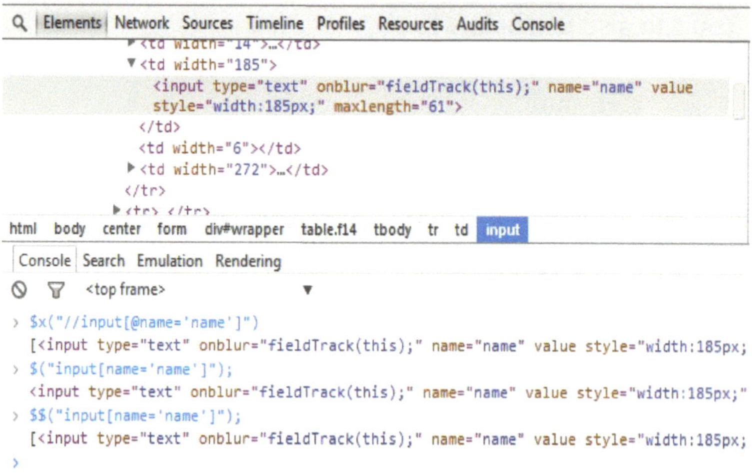

Figure 12 - Console window in chrome

To test xpath expressions, you can use below syntax.
`$x("//input[@name='name']")`

To test CSS expressions, you can use below syntax. $ will return only first matched element.
`$("input[name='name']")`

To test CSS expressions, you can use below syntax. $$ will return all matched elements.
`$$("input[name='name']")`

3.2.CSS

CSS selectors can also be used to find the web elements in a web page. You can visit
http://www.w3schools.com/cssref/css_selectors.asp to learn about css selectors.

```
IWebElement we =
driver.FindElement(By.CssSelector("#shadow"));

We.click();
```

Above code will identify the first element having id equal to "**shadow**" and then click on it.

Below table shows commonly used css Selectors in Selenium.

Find all elements with tag input	input
Find all input tag element having attribute type = 'hidden'	input[type='hidden']
Find all input tag element having attribute type = 'hidden' and name attribute = 'ren'	input[type='hidden'][name ='ren']
Find all input tag element with attribute type containing 'hid'	input[type*='hid']
Find all input tag element with attribute type starting with 'hid'	input[type^='hid']
Find all input tag element with attribute type ending with 'den'	input[type$='den']

3.3.LinkText

This method can be used to identify only links in the web page.

Example – Suppose you want to click on the link "news".
You can use below syntax to click on the link.

```
IWebElement we = driver.FindElement(By.LinkText
  ("news"));

We.click();
```

3.4.Name

This method can be used to identify any object in the web page.

Only requirement is that the object should have a name attribute associated with it.

Example – Suppose you want to click on the button with name "submit". You can use below syntax to click on the button.

```
IWebElement we =
driver.findElement(By.Name("submit"));
We.click();
```

3.5.Id

This method can be used to identify any object in the web page.

Only requirement is that the object should have a id attribute associated with it.

Example – Suppose you want to click on the button having id as "next". You can use below syntax to click on the button.

```
IWebElement we =
driver.findElement(By.Id("next"));
```

3.6.Class Name

This method can be used to identify any object in the web page.

Only requirement is that the object should have a class attribute associated with it.

Example – Suppose you want to click on the button having class as "highlight". You can use below syntax to click on the button.

```
IWebElement we =
driver.findElement(By.ClassName("highlight"));
```

3.7.Tag Name

This method can be used to identify any element in the web page with given tag.

Example – Suppose you want to click on the first link. You can use below code.

```
IWebElement we =
driver.findElement(By.TagName("A"));
```

3.8.Partial Link Text

This method can be used to identify only links in the web page.

Example – Suppose you want to click on the link with the text "google news". You can use below code.

```
IWebElement we =
driver.findElement(By.PartialLinkText("news"));
```

4. Performing User Actions in Selenium

> *In this chapter, you will learn how to enter the data in webpage controls like editbox, combobox and how to select controls like checkbox, radiobutton. You will also know how to click on links, buttons or any other web element using selenium webdriver in Java.*

Performing user actions involves identification of the elements on the webpage and then doing some operation like clicking on the button, entering the data in the editboxes, selecting a value from the drop down.

4.1. Entering data in Editboxes

We can enter the data in the editboxes using sendkeys method as illustrated in the below example.

```csharp
using System;
using System.Collections.Generic;
using System.Linq;
using System.Text;
using System.Threading;
using OpenQA.Selenium;

using OpenQA.Selenium.Firefox;
using OpenQA.Selenium.Chrome;
using OpenQA.Selenium.IE;
using OpenQA.Selenium.Support.UI;
using System.Collections.ObjectModel;
namespace Abc
{
    class Program
    {
```

```csharp
        static void Main(string[] args)
        {


IWebDriver driver=null;
try
{
driver = new
ChromeDriver(@"F:\selenium\csharp");
driver.Url = "http://www.google.co.in";


driver.Manage().Timeouts().ImplicitlyWait(TimeS
pan.FromSeconds(20));

driver.Navigate();

//enter data in google search box

driver.FindElement(By.XPath("//*[@id='lst-
ib']")).SendKeys("Selenium Book in C#");

        }

 catch(Exception e){
 Console.WriteLine("Exception
******"+e.ToString());

 }

        finally{
        Thread.Sleep(2000);
        driver.Quit();
        Console.ReadLine();
        }


    }
  }
}
```

4.2. Selecting a value from the Combo boxes.

We can select the value from the dropdown using 3
methods

1. SelectByText method
2. SelectByIndex method
3. SelectByValue method

You can use any of these methods to select a value from
the dropdown.

```csharp
using System;
using System.Collections.Generic;
using System.Linq;
using System.Text;
using System.Threading;
using OpenQA.Selenium;

using OpenQA.Selenium.Firefox;
using OpenQA.Selenium.Chrome;
using OpenQA.Selenium.IE;
using OpenQA.Selenium.Support.UI;
using System.Collections.ObjectModel;
namespace Abc
{
    class Program
    {
        static void Main(string[] args)
        {


IWebDriver driver=null;
try
```

```
{
driver = new
ChromeDriver(@"F:\selenium\csharp");
driver.Url = "http://www.amazon.in";


driver.Manage().Timeouts().ImplicitlyWait(TimeS
pan.FromSeconds(20));

driver.Navigate();

//enter data in google search box

IwebElement e = driver.FindElement(By.XPath
("//*[@id='searchDropdownBox']"));

SelectElement select=new SelectElement(e);

//select the value Books from the combo box
select.selectByText("Books");


            }

 catch(Exception e){
 Console.WriteLine("Exception
******"+e.ToString());

 }

            finally{
            Thread.Sleep(2000);
            driver.Quit();
            Console.ReadLine();
            }


        }
    }
}
```

4.3. Clicking on Web Buttons in

We can click on the buttons using click method as illustrated in the below example.

```csharp
using System;
using System.Collections.Generic;
using System.Linq;
using System.Text;
using System.Threading;
using OpenQA.Selenium;

using OpenQA.Selenium.Firefox;
using OpenQA.Selenium.Chrome;
using OpenQA.Selenium.IE;
using OpenQA.Selenium.Support.UI;
using System.Collections.ObjectModel;
namespace Abc
{
    class Program
    {
        static void Main(string[] args)
        {


IWebDriver driver=null;
try
{
driver = new
ChromeDriver(@"F:\selenium\csharp");
driver.Url = "http://www.amazon.in";
```

```
driver.Manage().Timeouts().ImplicitlyWait(TimeS
pan.FromSeconds(20));

driver.Navigate();

//enter data in google search box

IwebElement e = driver.FindElement(By.XPath
("//*[@id='twotabsearchtextbox']"));

e.SendKeys("Selenium");

IwebElement e1 = driver.FindElement(By.XPath
("//*[@id='nav-bar-
inner']/div/form/div[2]/input"));

//click on the button
     e1.click();

            }

 catch(Exception e){
 Console.WriteLine("Exception
******"+e.ToString());

 }

            finally{
            Thread.Sleep(2000);
            driver.Quit();
            Console.ReadLine();
            }


        }
    }
}
```

4.4.Clicking on links

We can click on the links using click method just like how we click on the buttons as illustrated in the below example.

```csharp
using System;
using System.Collections.Generic;
using System.Linq;
using System.Text;
using System.Threading;
using OpenQA.Selenium;

using OpenQA.Selenium.Firefox;
using OpenQA.Selenium.Chrome;
using OpenQA.Selenium.IE;
using OpenQA.Selenium.Support.UI;
using System.Collections.ObjectModel;
namespace Abc
{
    class Program
    {
        static void Main(string[] args)
        {


IWebDriver driver=null;
try
{
driver = new
ChromeDriver(@"F:\selenium\csharp");
driver.Url = "http://www.amazon.in";
```

```
driver.Manage().Timeouts().ImplicitlyWait(TimeS
pan.FromSeconds(20));

driver.Navigate();

//enter data in google search box

IwebElement e1 = driver.FindElement(By.LinkText
("sell"));

//click on the link sell

e1.click();



        }

 catch(Exception e){
 Console.WriteLine("Exception
******"+e.ToString());

 }

        finally{
        Thread.Sleep(2000);
        driver.Quit();
        Console.ReadLine();
        }


     }
    }
}
```

4.5.Setting on/off checkboxes

We can first see if the checkbox is selected using Selected property. Then using click method we can perform the operations such as selecting or deselecting the checkboxes as illustrated in the below example.

```csharp
using System;
using System.Collections.Generic;
using System.Linq;
using System.Text;
using System.Threading;
using OpenQA.Selenium;

using OpenQA.Selenium.Firefox;
using OpenQA.Selenium.Chrome;
using OpenQA.Selenium.IE;
using OpenQA.Selenium.Support.UI;
using System.Collections.ObjectModel;
namespace Abc
{
    class Program
    {
        static void Main(string[] args)
        {


IWebDriver driver=null;
try
{

driver = new
ChromeDriver(@"F:\selenium\csharp");

driver.Url = "https://www.gmail.com";

driver.Manage().Timeouts().ImplicitlyWait(TimeS
pan.FromSeconds(20));
```

```
driver.Navigate();

//enter data in google search box

IwebElement e1 = driver.FindElement(By.XPath
("//*[@id='PersistentCookie']"));

//click on the link sell


if (e1.Selected)
{

//deselect checkbox
e1.click();

}
else
{

//select checkbox
e1.click();

}

}

 catch(Exception e){
 Console.WriteLine("Exception
******"+e.ToString());

 }

        finally{
        Thread.Sleep(2000);
        driver.Quit();
        Console.ReadLine();
        }
```

```
            }
        }
}
```

4.6. Selecting the radiobutton

We can select the radiobutton using click method as illustrated in the below example.

```csharp
using System;
using System.Collections.Generic;
using System.Linq;
using System.Text;
using System.Threading;
using OpenQA.Selenium;

using OpenQA.Selenium.Firefox;
using OpenQA.Selenium.Chrome;
using OpenQA.Selenium.IE;
using OpenQA.Selenium.Support.UI;
using System.Collections.ObjectModel;
namespace Abc
{
    class Program
    {
        static void Main(string[] args)
        {


IWebDriver driver=null;
try
{

driver = new
ChromeDriver(@"F:\selenium\csharp");

driver.Url =
"http://register.rediff.com/register/register.p
hp";
```

```csharp
driver.Manage().Timeouts().ImplicitlyWait(TimeS
pan.FromSeconds(20));

driver.Navigate();

//select the radio button on rediff register
page

IwebElement e1 = driver.FindElement(By.XPath
("//*[@id='wrapper']/table[2]/tbody/tr[21]/td[3
]/input[2]"));

e1.Click();

}

  catch(Exception e){
  Console.WriteLine("Exception
******"+e.ToString());

 }

            finally{
            Thread.Sleep(2000);
            driver.Quit();
            Console.ReadLine();
            }


        }
    }
}
```

5. Reading data from webpage in Selenium

> *In this chapter, you will learn how to read the data from webpage controls like editboxes, comboboxes etc. You will also learn how to see if the elements are enabled, disabled and selected. You will also know how to read the data from table on webpage using selenium webdriver.*

Selenium C# API provides 2 important methods to read data from web elements.

1. **GetCssValue** – gets the value of css property of the element
2. **GetAttribute** – gets the value of given attribute.

We can also find the innertext of the element using **Text** property.

We can also check if

1. Element is displayed using **Displayed** property
2. Element is selected using **Selected** property
3. Element is enabled using **Enabled** property

Examples –

Below statement will print the width of the element having name login.

```
String x =
driver.FindElement(By.Name("login")).GetCssValu
e("width");
```

Below statement will print the value of the attribute onfocus of the element having name login.

```
String x =
driver.FindElement(By.Name("login")).GetAttribu
te("onfocus");
```

Below statement will print true if the checkbox with name choice is selected.

```
Boolean x =
driver.FindElement(By.Name("choice")).Selected(
);
```

Below statement will print true if the radiobutton with name Gender is displayed on the current webpage.

```
Boolean x =
driver.FindElement(By.Name("Gender")).Displayed
();
```

Below statement will print true if the button with name add is enabled.

```
Boolean x =
driver.FindElement(By.Name("add")).Enabled();
```

5.1.Reading data from Editboxes

We can get the data from editbox using GetAttribute
Method as illustrated in the below example.

```
using System;
using System.Collections.Generic;
using System.Linq;
using System.Text;
using System.Threading;
using OpenQA.Selenium;

using OpenQA.Selenium.Firefox;
using OpenQA.Selenium.Chrome;
using OpenQA.Selenium.IE;
using OpenQA.Selenium.Support.UI;
using System.Collections.ObjectModel;

namespace Abc
{
    class Program
    {
        static void Main(string[] args)
        {

            IWebDriver driver=null;
            try
            {
        driver = new
ChromeDriver(@"F:\selenium\csharp");
driver.Url =
"http://register.rediff.com/register/register.p
hp";


driver.Manage().Timeouts().ImplicitlyWait(TimeS
pan.FromSeconds(20));
```

```csharp
driver.Manage().Timeouts().SetPageLoadTimeout(TimeSpan.FromSeconds(50));


driver.Manage().Window.Maximize();
            driver.Navigate();

            IWebElement e=null;

            Thread.Sleep(1000);


            e =
driver.FindElement(By.Name("name"));
            e.SendKeys("sagar");



            Console.WriteLine("Text
displayed is -> " + e.GetAttribute("value"));


            Console.ReadLine();



        }
        catch(Exception e){

Console.WriteLine("Exception
....*********"+e.ToString());

        }

        finally{
        Thread.Sleep(2000);
        driver.Quit();
        Console.ReadLine();
        }
```

```
            }
        }
}
```

5.2.Reading data from combo boxes

We can get the data from combobox using Text property as illustrated in the below example.

```csharp
using System;
using System.Collections.Generic;
using System.Linq;
using System.Text;
using System.Threading;
using OpenQA.Selenium;

using OpenQA.Selenium.Firefox;
using OpenQA.Selenium.Chrome;
using OpenQA.Selenium.IE;
using OpenQA.Selenium.Support.UI;
using System.Collections.ObjectModel;

namespace Abc
{
    class Program
    {
        static void Main(string[] args)
        {

 //IWebDriver x = new
InternetExplorerDriver(@"F:\selenium\csharp");
 //IWebDriver x = new FirefoxDriver();
```

```
                IWebDriver driver=null;
                try
                {
        driver = new
ChromeDriver(@"F:\selenium\csharp");
                driver.Url =
"http://register.rediff.com/register/register.p
hp";


driver.Manage().Timeouts().ImplicitlyWait(TimeS
pan.FromSeconds(20));

driver.Manage().Timeouts().SetPageLoadTimeout(T
imeSpan.FromSeconds(50));

driver.Manage().Window.Maximize();
                driver.Navigate();

                IWebElement e=null;

                Thread.Sleep(5000);



//get the value selected in month drop down
rediff page.

            e =
driver.FindElement(By.Name("DOB_Month"));

                SelectElement se = new
SelectElement(e);


Console.WriteLine(se.SelectedOption.Text);

                Console.ReadLine();

```

```
        }
        catch(Exception e){

Console.WriteLine("Exception
....********"+e.ToString());

        }

        finally{
        Thread.Sleep(2000);
        driver.Quit();
        Console.ReadLine();
        }


      }
    }
}
```

5.3.Reading data from checkboxes

We can see if the checkbox is selected or not using
Selected property as illustrated in the below example.

```
using System;
using System.Collections.Generic;
using System.Linq;
using System.Text;
using System.Threading;
using OpenQA.Selenium;

using OpenQA.Selenium.Firefox;
using OpenQA.Selenium.Chrome;
using OpenQA.Selenium.IE;
using OpenQA.Selenium.Support.UI;
```

```
using System.Collections.ObjectModel;

namespace Abc
{
    class Program
    {
        static void Main(string[] args)
        {

            //IWebDriver x = new
InternetExplorerDriver(@"F:\selenium\csharp");
            //IWebDriver x = new
FirefoxDriver();
            IWebDriver driver=null;
            try
            {
        driver = new
ChromeDriver(@"F:\selenium\csharp");
                driver.Url =
"http://register.rediff.com/register/register.p
hp";


driver.Manage().Timeouts().ImplicitlyWait(TimeS
pan.FromSeconds(20));

driver.Manage().Timeouts().SetPageLoadTimeout(T
imeSpan.FromSeconds(50));

driver.Manage().Window.Maximize();
                driver.Navigate();

                IWebElement e=null;

                Thread.Sleep(5000);

//verify if checkbox is selected or not.

        e =
driver.FindElement(By.Name("chk_altemail"));
```

```
Console.WriteLine("Checkbox is selected ?" +
e.Selected);

                Console.ReadLine();

        }

        catch(Exception e){

Console.WriteLine("Exception
....*********"+e.ToString());

        }

        finally{
        Thread.Sleep(2000);
        driver.Quit();
        Console.ReadLine();
        }


        }
    }
}
```

5.4.Reading data from Radio Buttons

We can see if the radiobutton is selected or not using Selected property as illustrated in the below example.

```
using System;
using System.Collections.Generic;
using System.Linq;
using System.Text;
using System.Threading;
using OpenQA.Selenium;
```

```csharp
using OpenQA.Selenium.Firefox;
using OpenQA.Selenium.Chrome;
using OpenQA.Selenium.IE;
using OpenQA.Selenium.Support.UI;
using System.Collections.ObjectModel;

namespace Abc
{
    class Program
    {
        static void Main(string[] args)
        {

            //IWebDriver x = new
InternetExplorerDriver(@"F:\selenium\csharp");

            //IWebDriver x = new
FirefoxDriver();

            IWebDriver driver=null;
            try
            {
                driver = new
ChromeDriver(@"F:\selenium\csharp");
                driver.Url =
"http://register.rediff.com/register/register.p
hp";


driver.Manage().Timeouts().ImplicitlyWait(TimeS
pan.FromSeconds(20));

driver.Manage().Timeouts().SetPageLoadTimeout(T
imeSpan.FromSeconds(50));

driver.Manage().Window.Maximize();
                driver.Navigate();

                IWebElement e=null;
```

```
                Thread.Sleep(5000);

ReadOnlyCollection <IWebElement> ec =
driver.FindElements(By.Name("gender"));

for (int k=0;k<ec.Count;k++)
Console.WriteLine("which gender selected ?" +
ec[k].Selected);


                Console.ReadLine();



        }
        catch(Exception e){

Console.WriteLine("Exception ...*****" +
e.ToString());

        }

        finally{
        Thread.Sleep(2000);
        driver.Quit();
        Console.ReadLine();
        }


      }
    }
}
```

5.5.Working with Tables in SELENIUM

Reading the data from the table is very easy in selenium webdriver.

We can identify the table using name, Id or xpath and then we can access the rows one by one using findElements method.

For example – below statement will find all row elements from the given table. Please note that t stands for the table object you have found using findElement method.

ReadOnlyCollection <IWebElement> ec
= t.FindElements(By.TagName("tr"));

Another example – Below example illustrates how we can find the column number for the given column name in a table.

```csharp
int getColumnNumber (IWebElement r, String
columnName )
{

//get all the th elements from the page


ReadOnlyCollection <IWebElement> cells =
r.FindElements (By.TagName ("th"));
int c = 0;

for (int k=0;k<cells.Count;k++)
 c=c+1;
Console.WriteLine (c + " --> "+
cells[k].Text );

//return the column number of the column
name
```

```
 if (columnName.Equals(cells[k].Text))
break;
}

return c;
}
```

Another example – Below example illustrates how we can check if the value in given cell matches the desired value.

Below function takes 3 parameters. First parameter is row element. Second parameter is the column number and third parameter is expected value.

```
boolean verifyValue (IWebElement r, int a,
String expValue)
{

//get all the td elements from the page

ReadOnlyCollection <IWebElement> mcells =
r.FindElements(By.TagName("td"));

int c = 0;

for (int k=0;k<mcells.Count;k++)
c=c+1;
if (c==a)
{

//we can get the value inside cell using
Text property.

if (expValue.Equals(mcells[k].Text))
return true;
```

```
        }

      }
      return false;

    }
```

6. Synchronization in SELENIUM

In this chapter, you will learn how to add synchronization points in your selenium program using various methods. You will also know how to add explicit wait conditions. We can use below synchronization methods in selenium.

6.1. Page Load Synchronization

We can set the default page navigation timeout. Below statement will set the navigation timeout as 50. This means that selenium script will wait for maximum 50 seconds for page to load. If page does not load within 50 seconds, it will throw an exception.

```
driver.Manage().Timeouts().SetPageLoadTimeout(TimeSpan.FromSeconds(50));
```

6.2. Element Synchronization

We can set the default element existance timeout. Below statement will set the default object synchronization timeout as 20. This means that selenium script will wait for maximum 20 seconds for element to exist. If Web element does not exist within 20 seconds, it will throw an exception.

```
driver.manage().timeouts().implicitlyWait(20, TimeUnit.SECONDS);
```

6.3. Synchronization based upon specific condition

We can also instruct selenium to wait until element is in one of the expected conditions mentioned below.

1. ElementExists
2. ElementIsVisible
3. TitleContains
4. TitleIs

For example, below code will wait until the element with id – "dd" exists in the application. Timeout for this condition check is 20 seconds and while waiting driver will ignore the exceptions as coded in the second statement.

```
WebDriverWait w = new WebDriverWait(driver,
TimeSpan.FromSeconds(20));

w.IgnoreExceptionTypes(typeof(StaleElementRefer
enceException),typeof(InvalidElementStateExcept
ion));

w.Until(ExpectedConditions.ElementExists(By.Id(
"dd")));
```

7. Advanced Operations in Selenium

In this chapter, you will learn about how to perform complex mouse and keyboard events in Selenium. You will also get to know how to take screenshot and execute java script in Selenium Webdriver.

7.1. Mouse Events in SELENIUM

We can simulate many events in selenium using Actions class defined in using OpenQA.Selenium.Interactions namespace.

1. Click
2. ClickAndHold
3. ContextClick
4. DoubleClick
5. DragAndDrop
6. KeyUp
7. KeyDown

Double click on the given element

```
e = driver.FindElement(By.Name("showdetail"));

Actions a = new Actions(driver);
a.DoubleClick(e).Build().Perform();
```

Right click on the given element

```
e = driver.FindElement(By.Name("showdetail"));

Actions a = new Actions(driver);
```

```
a.ContextClick(e).Build().Perform();
```

7.2.Taking Screen shots in SELENIUM

Below code will illustrate how we can take screen shots in selenium in C#.Net.

```csharp
using System;
using System.Collections.Generic;
using System.Linq;
using System.Text;
using System.Threading;
using OpenQA.Selenium;

using OpenQA.Selenium.Firefox;
using OpenQA.Selenium.Chrome;
using OpenQA.Selenium.IE;
//for SelectElement
using OpenQA.Selenium.Support.UI;
using System.Collections.ObjectModel;
//for events - Actions
using OpenQA.Selenium.Interactions;
//for image format
using System.Drawing.Imaging;


namespace Abc
{
    class Program
    {
        static void Main(string[] args)
        {

            //IWebDriver x = new
InternetExplorerDriver(@"F:\selenium\csharp");
            //IWebDriver x = new
FirefoxDriver();

            IWebDriver driver=null;
```

```
 try
    {
                driver = new
ChromeDriver(@"F:\selenium\csharp");
                driver.Url =
"http://register.rediff.com/register/register.p
hp";


driver.Manage().Timeouts().ImplicitlyWait(TimeS
pan.FromSeconds(20));

driver.Manage().Timeouts().SetPageLoadTimeout(T
imeSpan.FromSeconds(50));

driver.Manage().Window.Maximize();
                driver.Navigate();

ITakesScreenshot screenshotDriver =
(ITakesScreenshot)driver;

                Screenshot screenshot =
screenshotDriver.GetScreenshot();

screenshot.SaveAsFile("d:\\photos\\abc.png",
ImageFormat.Png);

                //Console.ReadLine();

            }
            catch(Exception e){

Console.WriteLine("Exception
....********"+e.ToString());

            }

            finally{
            Thread.Sleep(2000);
```

```
        driver.Quit();
        // Console.ReadLine();
        }


    }
  }
}
```

7.3.Executing Java Script in SELENIUM

We can use Javascript Executor interface to execute script in Selenium.

JavascriptExecutor Executes JavaScript in the context of the currently selected frame or window. The script fragment provided will be executed as the body of an anonymous function. Within the script, use document to refer to the current document.

Note that local variables will not be available once the script has finished executing, though global variables will persist. If the script has a return value (i.e. if the script contains a return statement), then the following steps will be taken:

1. For an HTML element, this method returns a WebElement
2. For a decimal, a **Double** is returned
3. For a non-decimal number, a **Long** is returned
4. For a boolean, a **Boolean** is returned
5. For all other cases, a **String** is returned.
6. For an array, return a List with each object following the rules above. We support nested lists.
7. Unless the value is null or there is no return value, in which null is returned

Arguments must be a number, a boolean, a String, WebElement, or a List of any combination of the above. An exception will be thrown if the arguments do not meet these criteria. The arguments will be made available to the JavaScript via the "arguments" magic variable, as if the function were called via "Function.apply"

Below code will illustrate how we can execute Java script with webdriver in C#.Net.

```csharp
using System;
using System.Collections.Generic;
using System.Linq;
using System.Text;
using System.Threading;
using OpenQA.Selenium;

using OpenQA.Selenium.Firefox;
using OpenQA.Selenium.Chrome;
using OpenQA.Selenium.IE;
//for SelectElement
using OpenQA.Selenium.Support.UI;
using System.Collections.ObjectModel;
//for events - Actions
using OpenQA.Selenium.Interactions;
//screenshot
using System.Drawing.Imaging;


namespace Abc
{
    class Program
    {
        static void Main(string[] args)
        {

            //IWebDriver x = new
InternetExplorerDriver(@"F:\selenium\csharp");
```

```
        //IWebDriver x = new
FirefoxDriver();
        IWebDriver driver=null;




        try
        {
            driver = new
ChromeDriver(@"F:\selenium\csharp");
            driver.Url =
"http://register.rediff.com/register/register.p
hp";


driver.Manage().Timeouts().ImplicitlyWait(TimeS
pan.FromSeconds(20));

driver.Manage().Timeouts().SetPageLoadTimeout(T
imeSpan.FromSeconds(50));

driver.Manage().Window.Maximize();
            driver.Navigate();

 String t =
((IJavaScriptExecutor)driver).ExecuteScript("re
turn
document.documentElement.innerText;").ToString(
);

            Console.WriteLine(t);


        }
        catch(Exception e){

            Console.WriteLine("Exception
....*********"+e.ToString());
```

```
        }

        finally{
        Thread.Sleep(2000);
        driver.Quit();
        Console.ReadLine();
        }


    }
  }
}
```

7.4 Working with special keys in SELENIUM

Below code will illustrate how we can execute Java script with webdriver in C#.Net.

```
e = driver.FindElement(By.Name("showdetail"))
        e.SendKeys(Keys.Enter)
```

8. Frames, Alerts and Windows in SELENIUM

In this chapter, you will learn how to perform various mouse and keyboard operations like double click, right click, drag and drop etc. You will also learn how to take screenshot, how to execute javascript from selenium webdriver.

8.1 Handling Frames

To work with frames we need to switch to the frame and then perform the operation inside it. We can switch to the frame using 3 ways in C# selenium API.

1. Using frame Index
2. Using frame name
3. Identifying a frame by any other method like id, class etc.

For example -

```
driver.SwitchTo().Frame(1);
//Above code will switch to the first frame in
web page

e = driver.FindElement(By.Id("bpl"));
driver.SwitchTo().Frame(e);
//Above code will switch to the frame with id
bpl

driver.SwitchTo().Frame("f1");
//Above code will switch to the frame having
name - f1.
```

Once you switch to the desired frame, you can do rest of the operations the same way as you do in single document page.

8.2 Working with Alerts

We can handle alerts using **Alert class in C#.Net** Web Driver.

At first, we need to get the alert reference using below syntax.

```
Alert alert = driver.switchTo().alert()

IAlert alert = driver.SwitchTo().Alert();
```

Then we can click on Ok button using below syntax.

```
alert.Accept();
```

Then we can click on Cancel button using below syntax.

```
alert.Dismiss();
```

To get the text displayed in the alert, you can use Text Property

```
String text = alert.Text();
```

We can get the enter data in the editbox displayed inside
the alert using below code

```
driver.SwitchTo().Alert().SendKeys("abc");
```

8.3 Working with Multiple Browser Windows

Below code will show you how we can handle pop up
windows in selenium in C#.Net.

Ok. Now let us see how to work with the **mulitple
windows in Selenium C#.**

```
//**********************************************
*
//below statemewnt will click on link
// and it will open new window

driver.FindElement(By.Id("link")).Click();


  String popWindowHandle = "";


  //get the current window handles

  String mainWindow =
driver.CurrentWindowHandle;

  //get the collection of all open windows

ReadOnlyCollection<string> windowHandles =
driver.WindowHandles;

        foreach (string handle in windowHandles)
                {
                    if (handle != mainWindow)
                    {
```

```
                        popWindowHandle =
handle;
                    break;
                }
            }

//switch to new pop up window
// and perform any operation you want to
perform

driver.SwitchTo().Window(popWindowHandle);

//Print the title of new pop up window just
opened.
Console.WriteLine(driver.Title);
driver.Close();

//switch back to the original window
driver.SwitchTo().Window(mainWindow);
```

9. Important Built-in Functions in C#.Net.

> In this chapter, you will learn important built in classes and their methods in C#.Net to work with strings, files, date and time, Math etc.You will need these methods when doing validations and comparisons while doing functional testing of web applications.

9.1. Working with Strings in C#.Net

We must know below string operations while working with selenium.

```
//To find the length of the string
 Console.WriteLine("Length of sagar -> " +
"sagar".Length);

    //To find the n characters from the left
side
Console.WriteLine("Left 3 char of sagar -> " +
"sagar".Substring(0, 3));

//To find the last n characters of the string
Console.WriteLine("Last 2 char of sagar -> " +
"sagar".Substring("sagar".Length - 2, 2));

//To convert the string to upper case
Console.WriteLine("String - sagar salunke in
upper case is -> " + "sagar
salunke".ToUpper());

//To convert the string to lower case
```

```csharp
Console.WriteLine("String - SAGAR SALUNKE in
lower case is -> " + "SAGAR
SALUNKE".ToLower());

//To check if the string starts with specified
sub string
Console.WriteLine("String - sagar salunke
starts with sagar? -> " + "sagar
salunke".StartsWith("sagar"));

//How to replace the string with other string
Console.WriteLine("sagar salunke replaced by
ganesh salunke -> " + "sagar
salunke".Replace("sagar", "ganesh"));

//padding the string from right
Console.WriteLine("sagar padded by 10* -> " +
"sagar".PadRight(10, '*'));

//Check if the given substring exists in string
Console.WriteLine("sagar salunke contains
sagar?" + "sagar salunke".Contains("sagar"));

//check for the equality of the string
Console.WriteLine("Result of comparison of sa
with Sa -> " + "sa".Equals("Sa",
StringComparison.OrdinalIgnoreCase));


//join 2 string in array
String[] p = { "sachin", "tendulkar" };
Console.WriteLine("String after joining -> " +
String.Join(" ", p));

 //find the index of character any character
say a
Console.WriteLine("Index of a in sadffa -> " +
"sadffa".IndexOf('a'));

//convert the string to array
```

```csharp
char[] ar = "sagar".ToArray();
Console.WriteLine("String converted to array -
sagar -> " + ar[2]);

//split the string by any character say *
String [] s= "sa*gar".Split('*');
Console.WriteLine("sa*gar splitted with * ->" +
s[0]);
```

9.2. Working with Date and Time

In all banking projects, you will have to calculate the date differences or find the future or past date. So you must know how to do this in C#.Net.

```csharp
    //print current system time and date
    Console.WriteLine (DateTime.Now);

    //convert the string to date
    DateTime d = new DateTime();
    d = DateTime.Parse("09-jan-1986");

    //convert the string to date using
parseexact method
                    d =
DateTime.ParseExact("09/01/1986","dd/MM/yyyy",S
ystem.Globalization.CultureInfo.InvariantCultur
e);


    //Get future date and Change the date format
in c#
```

```
Console.WriteLine(d.Add(TimeSpan.FromDays(1)).T
oString("dd/MM/yyyy"));

  //Get past date and Change the date format in
c#

Console.WriteLine(d.Add(TimeSpan.FromDays(-
1)).ToString("dd/MM/yyyy"));
```

9.3. Working with Files and Folders

Creating text files in C# is very simple with the help of File Class. Below lines of code illustrate how we can read as well as append the text data to a file.

```
//Create text file
StreamWriter fi =
File.CreateText(@"d:\abc.txt");
fi.WriteLine("Sagar shivaji salunke");
fi.Close();

//read text file

Console.WriteLine(File.ReadAllText(@"d:\abc.txt
"));


//append data

StreamWriter f =
File.AppendText(@"d:\abc.txt");
f.WriteLine("Hello Baby");
f.Close();
```

9.4. Maths

Important Maths related methods provided in C#.Net are given below.

1. Round - rounds the number to specific number of decimals.
2. Pow - to find value of x^y.

```
Console.WriteLine(Math.Round(34.456, 2));
//output will be 34.46

Console.WriteLine(Math.Pow(2, 3));
//output will be 8.
```

10. Exception Handling in SELENIUM

In this chapter, you will learn how to handle exceptions that might occur while working with selenium webdriver in C#.Net.

10.1 Exception Handling in C#.Net

Exception handling involves handling unexpected conditions in the program.

For example – dividing any number by 0 throws the exception

```
try
   {
                        int b = 0;
                        int a = 2 / b;


   }

catch (Exception ex)
   {

Console.WriteLine("Exception Type ->"
+ex.GetType().ToString());

Console.WriteLine("Exception Source ->" +
ex.Source);

Console.WriteLine("Exception Stacktrace ->" +
ex.StackTrace);
```

```
        }
```

Executing above program will produce below output. As displayed in the output the DivideByZeroException is generated and stacktrace also show the line number in the source file where the exception occurred.

```
Exception Type ->System.DivideByZeroException
Exception Source ->Selenium-IE
Exception Stacktrace ->  at Selenium_IE.topics.doop() in F:\selenium\SeleniumDr
iver\Selenium-IE\topics.cs:line 148
```

Please remember that we can have many catch blocks after try block. Whenever exception occurs, it is thrown and caught by the catch block. In catch block we can write the code for recovery.

10.2 Exceptions in Selenium Webdriver

Below is the list of most commonly occuring exceptions When working with selenium webdriver.

1. ElementNotVisibleException
2. InvalidElementStateException
3. InvalidSelectorException
4. NoAlertPresentException
5. NoSuchElementException
6. NoSuchFrameException
7. NoSuchWindowException
8. StaleElementReferenceException

9. TimeoutException

10. UnhandledAlertException

Let us try to understand the meaning of each of these exceptions. We will also discuss on how to avoid these exceptions.

ElementNotVisibleException

This kind of exception occurs when the element you are trying to perform operation on is not visible. The style attribute – visibility of the element or it's parent is hidden. To avoid this kind of exception, ensure that element is visible. If you are not able to make the element visible, try to execute javascript on that element.

For example, below code will click on the element with id – s using javascript.

```
IWebElement we =
driver.FindElement(By.Id("s"));

((IJavascriptExecutor)
driver).executeScript("arguments[0].click();",w
e);
```

InvalidElementStateException

This kind of exception occurs when the element you are trying to perform operation on is in invalid state. There are many scenarios when this exception might occur.
For example Trying to invoke Clear() method on link will trigger this exception.
To avoid this exception, make sure that you are performing the correct operation on right element.

InvalidSelectorException

This kind of exception occurs when the xpath or css selector expression you are using to identify the element on the webpage is not correct by syntax.
For example – below statement will throw InvalidSelectorException

```
IWebElement x =
driver.FindElement(By.Xpath("Images[:]"));
```

NoAlertPresentException

This kind of exception occurs when the element you are trying to switch the alert which is not present on web page.
To avoid this error, ensure that alert is really present on the webpage before switching to it.

NoSuchElementException

This kind of exception occurs when the findElement method is not able to find the element by the given identification method.
 To avoid this exception make sure that css or xpath expression you are using is correct. Also ensure that you are on right page and element is really loaded in the webpage. Some elements take longer time to load. So try to add synchronization points before trying to find them.

NoSuchFrameException

This kind of exception occurs when the frame you are trying to switch to does not exist.

To avoid this exception make sure that css or xpath expression you are using is correct. Also ensure that you are on right page and frame is really loaded in the webpage.

NoSuchWindowException

This kind of exception occurs when the window you are trying to switch to does not exist.

To avoid this exception make sure that window you are trying to switch is really open and window handle you are using is also correct.

StaleElementReferenceException

This kind of exception occurs when the element you trying to perform operation on is removed and re-added to the web page. This usually happens when ajax changes your page source asynchronously. In other words, A StaleElementException is thrown when the element you were interacting is destroyed and then recreated using ajax.When this happens the reference to the element in the DOM that you previously had becomes stale and you are no longer able to use this reference to interact with the element in the DOM. When this happens you will need to refresh your reference, or in real world terms find the element again.

To avoid this exception, try to find the element again and again until you do not get StaleElementReferenceException.

TimeoutException

This kind of exception occurs when you use `WebDriverWait` to wait for some element.

UnhandledAlertException

This kind of exception occurs when alert is present on the webpage and you are trying to perform some operation on elements on the webpage.

11. Excel Programming in SELENIUM

> *In this chapter, you will learn how to read and write microsoft excel files in C#.Net*

C# provides a good support to do programming with Microsoft excel workbooks. You will have to add a reference of the excel library as shown in below figure.

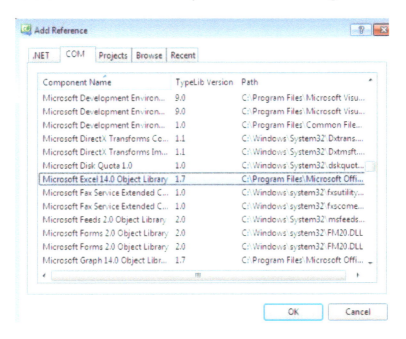

Figure 13 -Add reference of Excel Library

11.1. Creating and writing data to Excel Workbook

When we design a test automation framework in Selenium, we usually store the test data inside the excel sheets.Below example demonstrates how we can create and write to excel workbook.

We need to create an excel application reference as shown in below program. Then we can access native properties and methods of Excel Automation object.

```
try
  {

//Create the excel application object

Microsoft.Office.Interop.Excel.Application e =
new
Microsoft.Office.Interop.Excel.Application();

//make the excel visible

  e.Visible = true;

//Suppress the alert dialogs

  e.DisplayAlerts = false;

//add a new excel workbook
```

```
    Workbook wb = e.Workbooks.Add();

//get the reference of first sheet in workbook

    Worksheet ws = wb.Worksheets.get_Item(1);

//write some data to cell 1,1 (A1)
    ws.Cells[1, 1] = "salunke";

//save the workbook to d drive.

    wb.SaveAs(@"d:\csbook.xlsx");

//Close the excel workbook

    wb.Close();

//quit the excel application
    e.Quit();

    }

//handle excpetions if any.
catch(Exception ex){

Console.WriteLine("Exception Type ->"
+ex.GetType().ToString());

Console.WriteLine("Exception Source ->" +
ex.Source);

Console.WriteLine("Exception Stacktrace ->" +
ex.StackTrace);

                    }
```

11.2. Reading data from existing workbook

We usually store the test data in the Excel workbook. So we should know how to read it from the excel sheet. Below example shows how we can read the data from the excel sheets using below code.

```
try
         {
//Create the excel application object

Microsoft.Office.Interop.Excel.Application e =
new
Microsoft.Office.Interop.Excel.Application();

//make the excel application visible

   e.Visible = true;

//Suppress the excel alert dialogs

   e.DisplayAlerts = false;

//Open the excel workbook @ d:\csbook.xlsx

   wb = e.Workbooks.Open(@"d:\csbook.xlsx");

//get the first excel sheet from the workbook
   ws = wb.Worksheets.get_Item(1);

//Read the value in the cell A1 from sheet1
   Console.WriteLine("Data in cell 1,1 -> " +
(string)(ws.Cells[1, 1].Value));

//Close the workbook
   wb.Close();

//Quit the excel
```

```
   e.Quit();

 }
                       catch(Exception ex){

  Console.WriteLine("Exception Type ->"
+ex.GetType().ToString());

  Console.WriteLine("Exception Source ->" +
ex.Source);

  Console.WriteLine("Exception Stacktrace ->" +
ex.StackTrace);

                       }
```

12. Framework Designing in SELENIUM

In this chapter, you will learn about various automation testing frameworks in Selenium. You will also learn about how to design the keyword driven automation framework in C#.Net.

12.1 Frameworks in Selenium Webdriver

There are 3 types of automation frameworks that can be designed in selenium. Please note that In any other automation tools like QTP, Winrunner similar kinds of frameworks are popular.

Keyword Driven Framework :

In Keyword Driven Framework , Importance is given to functions than Test Data. when we have to test multiple functionality we can go for keyword frameworks. Each keyword is mapped to function in SELENIUM library and application.

DATA Driven Framework :

In data driven framework, importance is given to test data than multiple functionality of application. We design data driven framework to work with applications where we want to test same flow with different test data.

Hybrid Framework -

This is the combination of keyword and data driven frameworks.

After analyzing the application, you can decide what kind of framework best suits your needs and then you can design automation framework in SELENIUM.

12.2 Keyword driven framework in Selenium

Keyword driven automation framework is very popular among testing professionals. So in this section, I will explain you how to design the keyword driven automation framework.

It is very easy to design and learn a keyword driven automation framework in SELENIUM.

In this article I will explain you all the components of the keyword driven automation framework in SELENIUM with example. I will also explain the advantages and disadvantages of keyword driven automation framework in SELENIUM.

In keyword driven automation framework, focus is mainly on kewords/functions and not the test data. This means we focus on creating the functions that are mapped to the functionality of the application.

For example - Suppose you have a flight reservation application which provides many features like

1. Login to the application

2. Search Flights

3. Book Flight tickets

4. Cancel Tickets

5. Fax Order

6. View Reports

To implement the keyword driven automation framework for this kind of application we will create methods in C#.Net for each functionality mentioned above. We pass the test data and test object details to these functions.

The main components of keyword driven automation framework in SELENIUM

Each keyword driven automation framework has some common components as mentioned below.

1. Scripts Library

2. Test Data (generally in excel format)

3. SELENIUM - Settings and Environment Variables

4. Reports - (Generally in HTML format)

5. Test Driver Script Method

Test Data Sheet in keyword driven framework in SELENIUM.

Generally automated test cases are stored in excel sheets. From SELENIUM script ,we read excel file and then row by row we execute the functions in a test case. Each test case is implemented as a set of keywords.

Common columns in Data sheet are mentioned below.

1. Test case ID - Stores the Test Case ID mapped to Manual Test Cases.

2. Test Case Name - Name of the Test cases/ Scenario.

3. Execute Flag - if Marked Y -> Test case will be executed

4. Test_Step_Id - Steps in a test case

5. Keyword - Mapped to function in library file.

6. Object Types - Class of the object e.g winedit, webedit, swfbutton etc

7. Object Names -Names of objects in OR .

8. Object Values - Actual test data to be entered in the objects.

9. Parameter1 - This is used to control the execution flow in the function.

Test_ID	TC_Name	Execute	Test_Step_ID	Keyword	Object_Types	Object_Names	Object_Values	Parameter1
1	Login To App	Y	Step1	login	winedit.winedit	usend.password	salunke.mercury	
			Step2	Insert_Order	wincombobox wincombobo	flyfrom.flyto	london.paris	
			Step3	Fax_Order				Order_id

Please note that this is just a sample data sheet that can be used in keyword driven framework. There could be customized data sheets for each project depending upon the requirement and design.

For example there could be more parameters or test data is stored in the databases.

Test Driver Script in SELENIUM.

This is the heart of keyword driven / data driven frameworks. This is the main script that interacts with all modules mentioned above.

Main tasks that are accomplished by driver script are ->

1. Read data from the Environment variables.

2. Call report module to create Report folders / files

3. Read Excel file

4. Call the function mapped to keyword.

5. Log the result

13. Miscellaneous topics on SELENIUM

In this chapter, you will get to know about selenium ID and Selenium Grid. You will also learn about multi-browser testing, challenges and limitations of Selenium Webdriver.

13.1 Selenium IDE.

Selenium IDE is a Firefox plugin which records and plays back user interactions with the browser. Use this to either create simple scripts or assist in exploratory testing. You can also export the test scripts in languages like Java, C#, Ruby and Python.

You can install Selenium IDE xpi file from
http://release.seleniumhq.org/selenium-ide/

Follow below steps to install Selenium IDE

1. Open firefox browser
2. Go to tools -> Add-ons
3. Click on Gear icon ->Install add on from file
4. Browse xpi file downloaded from selenium site
5. Click on install now and restart Firefox

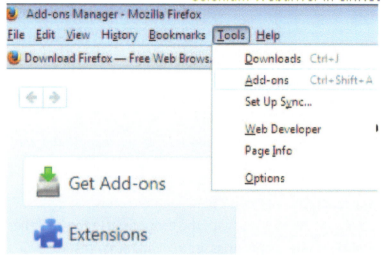

Figure 14 - Open Add-Ons page in Firefox

Click on the gear icon and then select Install Add-on From File...

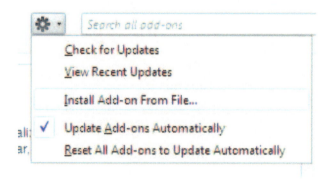

Figure 15 - Install Add-on from file

Then Browse to the selenium IDE xpi file downloaded from selenium website and select it. You will see next image.

Software Installation

⚠️ **Install add-ons only from authors whom you trust**

Malicious software can damage your computer or violate your priv

You have asked to install the following 5 items:

🧩 file:///G:/softwares/selenium/selenium-ide-2.5.0.xpi

🧩 **Selenium IDE** *(Author not verified)*
file:///G:/softwares/selenium/selenium-ide-2.5.0.xpi

🧩 **Selenium IDE: Python Formatters** *(Author not verified)*
file:///G:/softwares/selenium/selenium-ide-2.5.0.xpi

🧩 **Selenium IDE: C# Formatters** *(Author not verified)*

Install Now

Figure 16 - Install Selenium IDE add on

After you click on Install Now button, Add-on will be installed and you will have to restart the firefox. Then you will have to go to the Tools -> Selenium IDE to start it.

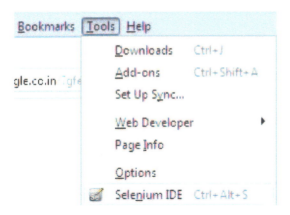

Figure 17 - Launch Selenium IDE in firefox

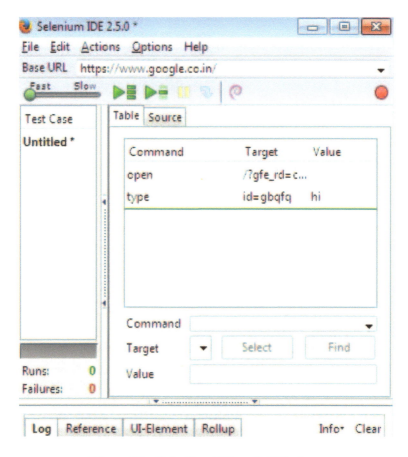

Figure 18 - Selenium IDE main Window

When you open selenium IDE, recording is automatically started. You can perform any operation on the web page open in firefox browser. As you can see in previuos figure, It shows the commands as we record it. We can export the test case in many languages as shown in next figure.

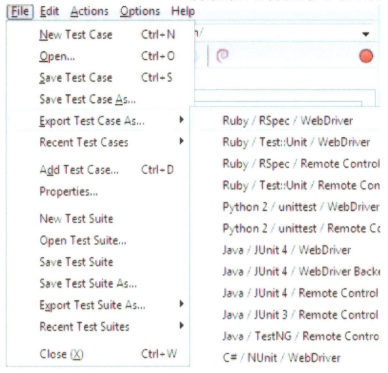

Figure 19 - Export test case in various languages

13.2 Selenium Grid.

Selenium Grid is used for running tests in parallel on different machines(called as nodes) from central machine(called as Hub).

Hub acts as a cental server. Based upon the configuration of the nodes (browser , OS), Hub will select the node and trigger the execution.

13.3 Multi-Browser Testing using Selenium.

Selenium webdriver is very popular tool to test cross-browser compatibility of the web applications.

The code you write for one browser say Firefox can be used as it is for other browsers like Internet Explorer, Chrome, Safari etc.

13.4 Limitations of Selenium Webdriver.

Below is the list of limitation of selenium.

1.   Selenium webdriver only supports testing of web applications.
2.   Desktop based applications developed in Java and .Net can not be automated using Selenium Webdriver
3.   We can not automate or verify the Flash Content, Silverlight Apps , Applet Contents using Selenium Webdriver.